Bob Kallestad
Bob Paulson

Norway

Visions & Verse of Vikingland

Norway

Visions and Verse of Vikingland

*The blue fjords and lush valleys beckon the
wanderer through these pages to pause and
"feel" the saga of this rugged and beautiful land.
The tapestry of people and places woven
together by the authors captures the "heart and
soul" of the Nordic Heritage.*

Robert Paulson • Robert Kallestad
Foreword by Bent Vanberg

Paulstad, Incorporated, Publishers • Minneapolis, Minnesota

ACKNOWLEDGEMENT

is gratefully given to our wives, Ruth and Joyce, who have given us
encouragement to carry this project through.

SPECIAL THANKS

to Bent Vanberg, Editorial Consultant to the Viking magazine, for his
assistance in the many details relating to Norwegian culture and
language.

NORWEGIAN SONGS

are from the Sons of Norway Song Book and are gratefully used with
the permission of The Supreme Lodge of the Sons of Norway,
Minneapolis, Minnesota.

CREDITS

Photography — Robert Paulson

Design, Art Production and Editorial — Vista III Design, Inc.
  Editor: Grant Gilderhus
  Art Director: Jerome Erickson
  Art Production: Ginger Root Gilderhus
                Tim Erickson

Color Separations — Riverside Litho, Inc.

Printing — Print Craft, Inc.

First published in the United States of America in 1981 by Paulstad, Inc.
2942 Kentucky Avenue North
Minneapolis, Minnesota 55427

Second printing, January 1982.

Library of Congress Catalog Card Number: 81-84961

ISBN: 0-9607344-0-6

Printed in the United States of America

dedicated

. . . to our parents, whose love for their heritage inspired us to be proud of it, and ultimately to go and search for a fuller understanding of it.

. . . to our relatives and friends in Norway who shared with us their homes and their hospitality.

. . . to those generations of Norse ancestors who have gone before, and whose visions and struggles have given us our legacy of the past.

. . . to the preservation of our Norwegian heritage and customs by renewing an interest in all those who are of Norwegian descent.

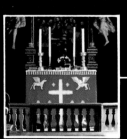

contents

foreword

"Wherever over rocks and hills you roam,
In winter or in summer gloam,
or where the waters foam,
From meadows and the towering pines,
From seashore and the fish confines
Out to the skerry lines,
View you the Land in the three-colors decked,
Colors from our flag their radiance reflect.

In the hillside the white, slender birches
Seem the patches of bluebells to seize,
At the roadside a red cottage perches,
It is the flag that is waved in the breeze.
Yes, as white as the snow in its whiteness,
And the red lends the sunset hue,
And the blue gave the glacier its brightness:
This is Norway in red, white and blue."

 This emotional new song swept throughout Norway during the never-to-be-forgotten year of 1945 when the people shook off the shackles of Nazi tyranny which had fettered them for five war-torn years.

Their existence had dragged drearily along since the land had been overrun in the calculated confrontation of 1940. Marred by hunger, imprisonment, executions and many other sufferings, the Norwegians had sought refuge and renewed encouragement in the old patriotic poems of great native poets. They found a new, often double, meaning in songs by beloved writers such as Bjørnstjerne Bjørnson, Henrik Ibsen, Henrik Wergeland, Arne Garborg, Jørgen Moe, Johan S. Welhaven, Per Sivle, Aasmund O. Vinje, Ivar Aasen and so many others who had added new dimensions to the treasures of national literature.

Again these songs — so many dealing with and praising Mother Norway herself and her saga from the dawn of the Viking age down to contemporary times — swelled in their hearts and burst forth on their lips. In addition, the spirit of the suppressed Norwegians was sustained by songs smuggled into the country, which were written by compatriots in exile, such as Nordahl Grieg, who was shot down over Berlin on New Year's Eve 1944 during an allied air raid.

Likewise, poetry and song buoyed up the Norwegians who became a part of the vast westward emigration, seeking a new life in a new world. They settled in strange surroundings, which in most cases were completely different from those in which they spent their childhood and youth.

Included in their meager worldly possessions were their family bibles, hymnals and song books filled with cherished poems they knew so well. Most of all they loved the songs telling of the land itself, which they had been forced to leave. They now sang these songs wherever they were: at home, in the fields, in the factories and workshops, in churches and schools. They sang them while lumberjacking, sailing, fishing, crossing prairies and mountains; and as they sang them, their native land again loomed before their inner eyes.

Yet, no poem, however beautifully formed in lines and rhymes by the great gallery of Norwegian lyricists, may ever be comparable to the one created by Norway herself in all her splendid scenery: an ode carved in the mighty majestic mountains to the west and north, with stanzas carried by the waves of the deep, narrow fjords and the winds breezing through the dark forests and along the fertile fields of verdant valleys. Through the verses are perceived the thunder of the roaring waterfalls and the whisper of the breezes from sunrise to sunset as the seasons shift.

This poem which may aptly be called "The Voice of Norway", never written, yet always there for thousands of years, was also ringing in the minds of these emigrating people. Most of them knew they would never again see the land of the midnight sun, but no one could ever deprive them of the magic visions of a scenic past as their voices rose in song. Thus, they and their descendants combined poems and mental pictures.

What is rather surprising is that, up to now, no picture book about Norway, however beautiful in glorious colors, has included selected poems most fittingly accompanying scenes of the land and people.

This present volume has, in an impressive and enriching way, corrected this situation. Now we can not only, in the words of President Franklin Roosevelt from his 1942 war-time speech, "Look to Norway," but also "Listen to Norway"! These two Americans of solid Norwegian stock, Robert Paulson and Robert Kallestad, fully deserve our gratitude and admiration for their personal initiative and professional effort in producing this memorable salute to their heritage.

Bent Vanberg

home & heritage

kulturarv & hjem

Independence! Freedom! The right to live and be what you are as a people, and to celebrate it. That is what *Syttende Mai* (Seventeenth of May) is to the people of Norway. These joyous moments were caught on the streets of Bergen where we joined in the festivities. For the very young, the very old and all those in between it is a special day . . . a day of being proud of their country, their heritage and their freedom. It was also evident that they are intensely proud of each other and what they are together as a nation of people.

Protect each maid and man, Forever more.

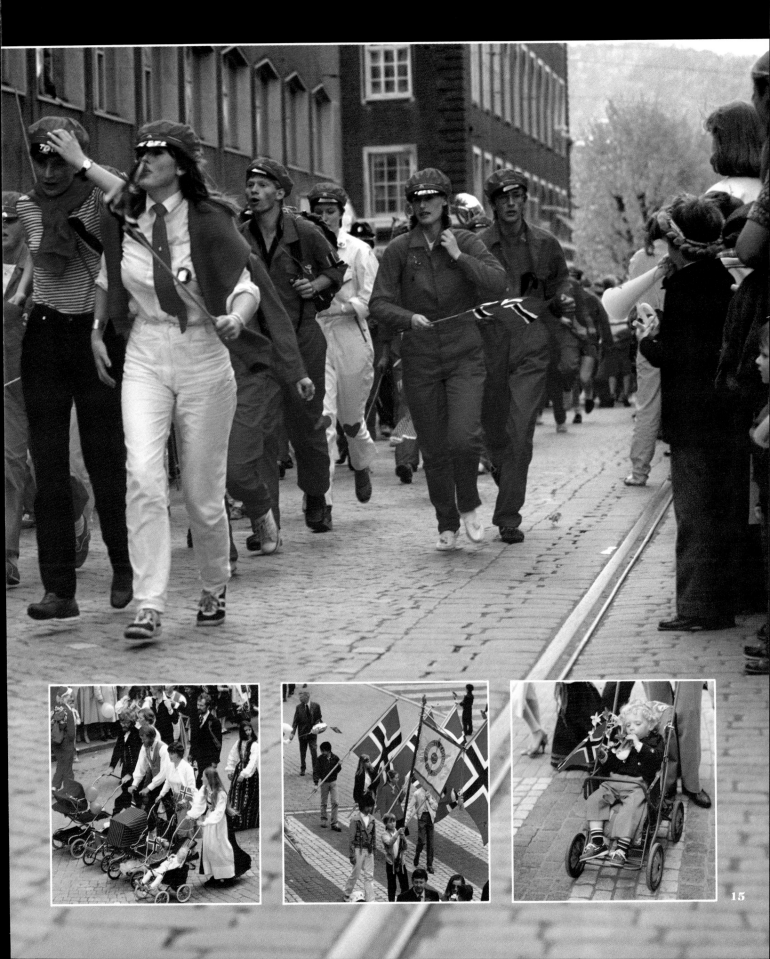

15

Heritage and tradition are celebrated on special days, but they live and grow in the hearts and homes of the people every day of the year. Green birch branches on the cars are typical of *Syttende Mai;* they speak of a new life and a new nation. But so also do the flowers that are a part of almost every home and cottage.

At bottom right is the home of Edvard Grieg, Norway's best known composer and certainly a part of the country's great heritage.

O, Sons of Norway,
That old, sturdy Nation,
Sing with harp now
a true festive song!
Sing to your country,
yes, shout with elation,
Lift up your voices,
rejoice and be strong.

Hospitality and home are synonymous with Norway. The warm glow of the little inn at Røsheim (left) is a memory we will cherish. The innkeeper, Signe Moland, was a most gracious lady who made us feel like we were part of her family...so much so that we hated to leave.

We found ourselves looking for other scenes that were typical of this simple and inviting warmth: the rustic log construction, the well swept hearth and even the cutting of wood for the family fire, which we chanced upon in Kaldestad.

We like to roam, but our home is best,
Home forever!
It has no equal in east or west,
Home forever!
Here round about things
are good and right
And over all is a gracious light,
Home forever!

Uff Da! I have never eaten so much in my life. Food is the "stuff" of hospitality in the Norwegian home. Many of these foods are known as traditional foods of Norway, and we certainly ate our fill while we were there. At the bottom of the page is a bowl of *rømmegraut,* a rich delicacy of thick cream. Opposite are the lovely open faced sandwiches *(smørbrød)* which are the daily fare wherever you go.

The socks on the line caught our eye because they just seemed to say "family".

Upon this hillock I safely dwell,
Home forever!
This home my father did build so well,
Home forever!

fjords & harbors

fjorder & havner

The fjords are a natural phenomena and a scenic wonder found in Norway. They are long fingers of the sea reaching inland through the mountains, and bringing the sea to almost every town and village in the western part of the country. The left page photo and the tourist ship were taken on our trip up the Geirangerfjord. The small inset is the town of Stryn nestled at the edge of Innviksfjorden.

When rivers are flowing
Unfettered and free,
And birds in the branches
Are warbling with glee
I murmur this pray'r
As enchanted I stand
God bless thee, Old Norway,
My beautiful land.

Faces are an interesting study in the land of the fjords. The faces of the men are bold and resolute, and seem to indicate great strength of character. The water has many faces; this day west of Bergen it was still and reflective. Even the faces of the buildings have a grace and beauty in their age; the facade opposite was along the waterfront in Trondheim.

28

There quivers a glittering summer air,
Warm over Hardangerfjord's fountains,
Where high 'gainst the heavens,
So blue and so bare.

Are tow'ring the mighty mountains.
The glacier shines so bright, the hillside is green,
All nature responds with beauty serene.
so blue and so bare.

Almost everywhere you go in Norway you are not far from fishermen and their intimate oneness with the sea. At once there seemed to be a loneliness and also a danger to this relationship between man and water. It could be seen in the lone trawler on Hardangerfjord, the man alone in his boat, and in the face of the fisherman waiting to return again to his beloved. . .the sea. And over it all, always the haunting cry of the gull. . .

On the deck I stand at night,
When the stars are bright;
Far away from friends and home,
Lonely here I roam.

The land, the buildings, the boats and the water seemed to be woven into one beautiful tapestry called "The Fjord". Each shape and texture became an important part of the whole. The lovely scene at left is near Grotnes; the boat was near Kaldestad. On this page we see a fisherman's combination house and boathouse near Televåg.

In some countries a school field trip usually entails a journey on a school bus. In Norway it can often be a journey by boat. The bright colors of the children wearing their life vests added a gaiety to the gray day as they came down the wharf to meet their boat in Runde. We joined them for a trip to the bird sanctuary, a haven for the fabled cormorants and puffins. These birds flock to this island because of the plentiful supply of fish which is their main food. It was a day to remember, including helping several young people who were a bit "sick" of the sea.

I seem to hear
the sound of children's voices
And dim with happy tears
spellbound I stand.
Each mem'ry of the past
my heart rejoices.

Spring on the fjords tells its own story; one of delicate greens, soft fragrant blossoms and wildflowers in abundance. Left is Geirangerfjord and the apple trees here are along Hardangerfjord.

Beautiful is spring in Norway's valleys;
Glorious victory nature here has had.
Earth awakens from its lengthy slumber;
Soon the hillsides are with flowers clad.

Norwegian seamen are a folk grown strong 'neath sail and spar
Where boats can find a way, the best men are they
On high seas or at home, in calm or when the stormwaves foam.

Along the edge of the fjord, especially, we became aware of the effect of wave, wind and weather on every surface they touch. This is but a glimpse of our recollections of these surfaces and shapes.

We wander and sing with glee
Of glorious Norway fair to see.
On mountain, forest, fjord and shore,
'Neath heaven's azure arching o'er.

44

The environs of the fjord and streams are for play as well as work. As we traveled we found the people enjoying many forms of outdoor recreation. While visiting Bob Paulson's relatives near Lundamo we were able to join them for the spring salmon fishing (opposite page). This freshly caught prize will provide many meals for the family.

arts & artists

kunst & kunstnere

You toil so hard, my mother dear,
Your heart is warm and full of cheer ...

The fabric arts have played a large part in the Norwegian life and heritage. We became acquainted with a weaver, Aud Sunde, and spent many pleasant hours with her while learning about her craft. The full photo of her hands at the loom (previous page) tells a love story of the artist and her art.

Whether contemporary or traditional, the designs are handsome and the colors bold and vibrant. We thought it fitting to include this montage of fabric variations on a theme.

*As monuments they yet shall stand
And show where lay my fatherland*

From the times of the Vikings the arts have been a part of the architecture of Norway. Today murals of steel, tile and wood adorn these buldings in Oslo (opposite page). Other arts are apparent in many shops and homes; glassware and woodcarving are some of the most well known.

On this page we recorded our visit with Toralf Flatjord near Skei. His studio is indoors or outdoors as he chooses, but his indoor studio would be the envy of any artist. It is a log cabin which is over 300 years old, yet in its simplicity it looks quite contemporary. His wonderful lyric abstractions of nature seem to be alive with the motion of clouds, leaves and water and we were privileged to share some time with him as he painted on location.

55

field & farm

jord & bruk

Although these pictures of milk from farm to market were taken in three different places (Lundamo, Voss and Dale), we thought they told a story of rural life in this beautiful country. The flowers which abound in these pastures in spring add sweetness to the vision, if not also to the milk.

Norway,
My Norway!
Let springtime appear
With sunshine
And warmth
For the meadows.

were our love but enough for the task to be done.

63

The farms and fields of Norway seemed alive with color when we were there. It inspired us to rejoice in the "aliveness" around us, and also prompted Bob Kallestad to make friends with some of the local inhabitants.

On the mountain!
The slope is cover'd with shining flow'rs,
The sunshine bathes them in golden show'rs,
On the mountain!

Perhaps it is because the farms in Norway are very small that we were so close to animals. Each turn of the road brought animals within reach, and it often seemed as if they were pets instead of livestock.

And then there were always the children . . . in the midst of the countryside, along the roads and always unexpectedly become a friendly part of our experience.

This is our homestead, and more
We are loving it for
What it was, what it is,
what the future will show.

Here's a land
of great beauty
so vast and so wide,
And I love it,
yes I love it,
Yes I love it
because
it is mine.

energy & enterprise

energi & tiltak

But when I consider the people who toil,
For humble reward from the sea or the soil;
The thousands who labor in country and town,
And weave for the brow of old Norway a crown;
I shout as my hat I exultantly wave:
Hurrah for my people so sturdy and brave!

Trees literally cover the slopes of the mountains and are certainly one of the great resources of the country. This lumber mill in Dale was a marvel of activity as logs were hauled, cut, piled and processed for a hundred different uses. We could have stayed longer and kept busy shooting photos from morning 'till night . . . alas we had to move on.

The art of the wooden barrel . . . finely tuned eyes select just the right pieces for a barrel and assemble them into the perfection of a circle. An ancient skill which made kegs for the Vikings is still in demand for many modern uses. It should be noted, however, that the skill has grown scarce and today wooden barrels are made only a few places in the world. It was a joy to try and capture the essence of a true craftsman at work . . . with only camera and film. It was also a joy to learn that there are a few places where loving care is still the only way to do the job.

Here is will to aspire
Through our work,
and desire

To be up and to do is his glory;
And he has to be sturdy and strong;
But 'tis pleasure to hear the old story,
Of the deeds that are treasured in song.

The abundance of trees provides one of Norway's most basic necessities . . . the boat. The art of wooden boat making is alive and at work as an everyday craft in this country which depends so much on the sea. There are not as many boatmakers as there used to be, but the oldtimers will tell you that a wooden boat is still the best. These "how to" pictures were taken at the boatworks of Andor Tveit in Sunde. We could quickly tell that the most important ingredient of boatmaking is the master's touch as he "feels" the boat begin to take shape.

But fishing boats in need-
Have shown so many
a daring deed
Of courage fine and skill,
Though unrecorded still.

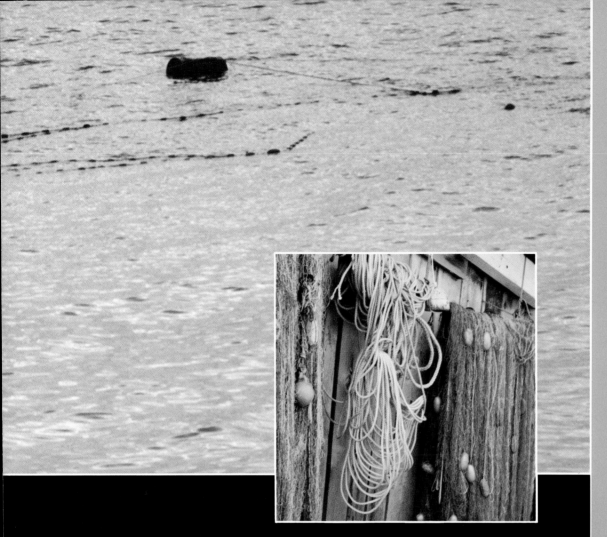

Fishing is *the* industry along the coast. They eat them, pack them, can them, dry them, export them and much more. The men, the boats and the nets were a constant source of fascination to us. The fisherman across the top of these pages was shot at Vik on a glary but overcast day. The fish vendor in the colorful coat was in Bergen and the fishermen in their boathouse were Oskar and Andreas Kvernevit of Flatraket.

Oft hard is life for the fisherman,
In icy waves he to splash is banished,
Ere cocks the day to proclaim began;
Of home he thinks not ere sun has vanished.
The rain is pouring, The storm is roaring.

See sloping the skerried coasts,
With gulls and whales and fishing-posts
And vessels in shelter riding,
While boats o'er the sea are gliding,
And nets in fjord and seines in sound,
And white with spawn the oceans ground.

*. . . and have toiled
in the sweat
of their brow.*

The old expression "tighter than sardines in a can" takes on new meaning when you stand in the canning factory and watch them pack 'em in (left bottom). The dried fish being stacked in piles were seen at another processing facility at Måløy.

church & faith

kirke & tro

To open one's book 'tis useless to try,
And psalms out of doors begin singing;
So distant my loft, 'twould seem, here on high
That tones become poor while they're ringing.
Ah, happy the one whose voice could in song
With his and the others be blending!
God grant that the harvest come before long,
My flock and myself homeward sending.

The churchyards, we found, were an endless store of history going back more years than even the stones can remember. The little church in Husnes at top left was a lovely setting with its well kept yard and wonderful trees.

Some of the history held by the stones and markers must be felt and absorbed in the spirit of the place because the stones bear no markings but the cross and the moss. Standing alone in the churchyard we could not help but wonder about the struggles and mishaps which may have befallen our ancestors.

The churches themselves are a storehouse of art treasures which are masterpieces from past centuries. At the bottom of this page is the altarpiece from the church in Ulvik, which is typical of the ageless beauty in these works.

93

The stave churches *(stavkirker)* are a heritage from the times which mark the end of the Viking era and the beginning of the Christian era in Norway. There were about twelve hundred of them built, of which only a handful remain to tell the story, like this classic example at Vik (left page).

Other churches represent other periods and styles of the country's history and were a colorful delight to the photographer's eye, such as the rural church at Lom (upper right).

I gaze on the sun;
It mounts in the skies.
The hour for Mass will soon be breaking
Ah, would I be home
'Midst all that I prize,
'Mong folks now the churchward path taking!

95

town & country

by & bygd

Grand above all else is spirit's springtime,
Freedom's birth the people has aroused.
Thus to Norway the task has given
Great and noble thoughts to be espoused.
Freedom's sun released the chains of winter,
Gave unto each nook its life and zest;
Heaven over all its plenty yielding,
Will to do and dare in ev'ry breast.

The hustle and bustle of the city was a nice change of pace from all our rural travels . . . perhaps it somehow felt more like home. While the aesthetics of photographing the quaint, the weathered and the picturesque had occupied most of our time (and film), it should be said that Norway is a modern and progressive country. This can be seen easily in the cities with their new modern buildings and industrial centers, such as Bergen and Oslo (opposite page). The flower market in Oslo was a riot of color and activity, becoming for us the "garden spot" of the city that day.

This amiable man on the bicycle is Jacob Runde who operates the boarding house *(pensjonat)* in the town of Runde on the island of Runde. He proved to be a fine host and became another square in the quilt of memories we were putting together.

Scenes on the opposite page are typical of much of the rural countryside where we traveled.

Heigh-o! how bracing the air and light,
On the mountain!
The wind here frolics in mad delight,
On the mountain!
The foot trips lightly, the eye it laughs,
The heart new life and enjoyment quaffs,
On the mountain!

And as love grows apace
On the cherished home place,
From the seed of our love
It shall constantly grow.

In spring when the fjords are like violets blue,
And glaciers in sunshine are golden in hue,
Lilies and roses their beauty combine,

The lush farms and beautiful valleys are a never ending source of visual poetry, like this pastoral scene near Lundamo on the opposite page. It must be a true joy to live this close to nature and to experience the wonders of her beauty every day. Many of the homes we saw had been situated to take the best advantage of their visual surroundings.

As we drove up through the hills and valleys we found ourselves so taken with the wonder of it all, that sometimes we forgot to record the location in our log for future reference. So it was in this "nameless" valley where we took time to explore a remote ravine. It was here that we chanced upon the trolls, the little elves which "inhabit" the unseen places of the countryside. We counted this as one of the great moments of the trip . . .many of the natives can only believe what they have heard about these elusive "little people".

The opposite page is a waterfall which tumbled over the crags and ledges of a wooded glen in the area of Stardalen near Skei.

**For the mountain I saw in my childhood is best:
I am proud of my fair fatherland.**

Norway, Norway! Houses and huts,
No castles grand, gentle or hard,
Thee we guard, thee we guard,
Thee our futures fair land.

Although you don't see many of them any more, the sod roofed house was once a very traditional style of building in Norway. Perhaps the people are not continuing the tradition because it is "going to the dogs".

The house on this page may not be the average architecture of most homes, but it certainly was an interesting one . . . and one we couldn't pass by without a couple of shots. Nor could we pass up recording these young girls with whom we became acquainted during our stay at Vik.

54 Gullbrå   569 Dale

113

It is ultimately the people who make the difference in visiting almost anywhere. You can enjoy the scenery, but without warm and friendly people who shared their hospitality and their homes, the trip would have been ordinary at best.

Our many warm memories of the people of Norway include the soccer players in Dale and school children in Bergen . . . including those who were waiting for the school bus (opposite). And the nursery school children were a delight to be with as we got to know them.

We wander and sing with glee
Of glorious Norway fair to see...
Our future shall be sure and bright,
As God we trust and do the right.

The faces . . . those we talked with, those we laughed with, those we lived with and those we only chanced to see in passing . . . all of them are now a permanent part of our visual tapestry which we take home on film. We also take them home in our hearts and cherish them with the hope that we may, perhaps, meet again someday.

Near and dear to all Norwegians, and to our memories of these people is the traditional dress *(bunad)* worn on holidays and special times to celebrate their heritage. It is the vision that will return to mind many times as we recall our stay in our ''homeland''.

Yes, we love this land of ours
As with mountain domes
Storm lash'd o'er the sea
it towers
With the thousand homes.
Love it dearly, ever thinking
Of our fathers' strife
And the land of Saga sinking,
Dreams upon our life,
And the land of Saga sinking,

Ja, vi elsker dette la
som det stiger frem
furet vaerbitt
over vannet
med de tusen hjem,
elsker, elsker det og
på vår far og mor
og den saganatt som
drømme på vår jord
og den saganatt som

the authors

ROBERT PAULSON

Although his heritage is Norwegian, "Bob" is from Minneapolis where he graduated from Washburn High School and went on to graduate from Augsburg College. He also studied at the University of Minnesota, Macalester College and the Minneapolis School of Art.

Bob has worked in photography since he was in school and has been with several studios. He now owns North Star Photography, a commercial studio located in St. Louis Park.

"My special interest is the 'design' aspect of the subjects I photograph," muses Bob. "I work at drawing out the relationships between strong shapes and contrasting areas of light and dark."

He has exhibited his work at the Minnesota State Fair, The Windsong Gallery in Nisswa, Minnesota and the Kelton Gallery in Dillon, Colorado. The Edina Art Center in Edina, Minnesota held an invitational one man show of his work, and in addition, Bob has won awards for several of his pictures.

A special privilege was to be named Official Photographer for the visits of King Olaf of Norway to the Twin Cities in both 1968 and 1975.

Travel, along with skiing and watercolor painting, has been one of Bob's favorite activities. Although he has traveled widely, he saved this trip to Norway until he would have the time to work on this long anticipated project.

This book is the culmination of years of thinking and planning toward a meaningful contribution to the understanding and preservation of his Norwegian heritage. The commentary in the vertical columns throughout the book is a digest of the trip "log" kept by the authors.

ROBERT KALLESTAD

This Bob was also born in Minneapolis but both of his parents were born in Norway and immigrated from the community of Kaldestad during those difficult economic times of the early 1900's.

He was a classmate of Bob Paulson's through elementary and junior high school when his parents moved to the Seattle, Washington area. Bob graduated from South Kitsap High School in Port Orchard, Washington.

Bob returned to Minneapolis and after serving a "hitch" in the U.S. Navy was employed as a helper in a print shop and later worked his way up to a pressman. In 1962 he borrowed money from his parents to buy a small second hand offset press to use in their basement for the purpose of supplementing the family income. "For this I owe a great deal to my parents," says Bob.

Since then his business, Print Craft, Inc. has grown to a thoroughly modern plant which employs over thirty people.

For Bob it was the fulfillment of a lifelong dream to go to Norway and visit the homes his parents lived in. "I still have relatives living in these same houses, and in the area along the Hardangerfjord," says Bob, "and it was a great thrill to be there in the land of my parents."

Publishing a book like this has been a thought in the back of his mind for a number of years; now his lifelong friendship with Bob Paulson has made it a reality for both of them. "We hope this book will, in some way, renew or create an interest in the heritage of those who are of Norwegian descent," reflects Bob.